THE ART OF APPLEWOOD

FROM HOSPITAL TO HOMES

RUTH DAVEY & LIS PARKER

FOREWORD BY KEVIN McCLOUD

DEDICATION

TO THE SPIRIT *of* THE LAND

First published by Look Again in 2014

www.look-again.org

Publication: © Ruth Davey and Lis Parker 2014
Photography: © Ruth Davey 2014
Design: © Chris J Bailey 2014
Print: Gemini West

ISBN No: 978-0-9931353-0-9

A CIP catalogue record for this book is available from the British Library.

Title page: View of the Cashes Green Hospital, circa 1910

ACKNOWLEDGEMENTS

This book would not have been possible without all the support, advice and financial backing offered by the various project partners (see Appendix 2). A special thanks goes to Kevin McCloud for writing the foreword and for fully supporting the book; to Sahra Gott for her belief and trust in us and for always being at the end of the phone; Mike Roberts, Simon McWhirter and Nick Taylor for their continued communication and patience; Denis Higgs for his unwavering cheer even when things got really tough; Sarah Button, for her lateral thinking, commitment and creativity; David Warburton for his enthusiasm that ensured we could move ahead financially; Kirsty Powell for encouraging the financial input from other contractors; Howard Beard for use of the archived photographs of the hospital; Chas Townley and Philip Booth for their local knowledge; Stroud News and Journal, for permission to use the article on page 4; Ruby, Dawn, Liz, Tessa, and Bryan for agreeing to be interviewed and photographed; Christine for her poem; those who attended the art workshop and submitted their work for inclusion in the book; Lorna Howarth from The Write Factor for her very helpful editorial overview; Chris Bailey for 'getting' the book and creating a fab design; Sue Everson for her advice regarding print; and lastly but by no means least, we would like to thank our families and in particular Dave and Yusupha for their continued patience and encouragement over the last two years.

CONTENTS

FOREWORD

Building is not easy. It is a process fraught with compromise and difficulty, where every day demands renewed energy to resist the onslaught of mud and mediocrity. To take on a site and work with the community and with partners to fight bureaucratic pettiness and bland building standards demands stamina and a certain belligerence. You need genius too; great design and brilliant ideas are sharp weapons.

But it is worth making the effort to resist the compromise, wage the battles and to champion quality. That way we prove that better is possible. Applewood did not just happen; it was argued over, fought for and dreamed of. It emerged as an idea through the work of Gloucestershire Land for People (GLP) and was developed into a somewhat fixed scheme by the Homes and Communities Agency (HCA). Haboakus entered a competition to build it and, on winning, learned that a lot more work needed to be done in the community. So, in no small way, and with the blessing of David Warburton at the HCA, we started again: to canvas people's views, collaborate with the parish, reform the idea in partnership and begin that fight against mediocrity.

When we founded HAB (which stands for Happiness, Architecture, Beauty) in 2007, a founding tenet was the belief in local distinctiveness – the idea that every place on the planet has a unique set of qualities in its geology, local history, weather, flora and fauna, and people. The best buildings, in my view, embody and contribute to that distinctiveness. The Cashes Green Hospital site provided us with it in the existing (if dilapidated) buildings, in the local badger, bat and slow-worm populations, in the allotments, in the sloping site, the red bricks of the neighbourhood and in the feisty, energetic engagement of the neighbourhood and Parish Council.

This book celebrates some of the successes and marks some of the losses. It records the passion of people who have poured their souls into a building project and staked their professional reputations to it; but equally importantly, the book brings together remembered events from people who have a long association with Cashes Green and the hospital. That makes it properly rich and resonant and that is in no small part, due to the years of work put in by Lis Parker and Ruth Davey alongside the important community research conducted by Rose Seagrief when at GLP. The book charts the history of the site not just with maps and dry historical documents but also with photographs

and stories. It brings together voices, which would otherwise be lost, to make something coherent and lasting from people's memories. It explains the context of Cashes Green and indeed assembles that context. And, like all good buildings, it goes on to become part of the evolving context of a new place, now called Applewood.

Stories are not just snippets of entertainment. They give us, and where we live, identity. They provide the warp and weft of our lives and hold our communities together. Through stories we gain our sense of connection to a place and make sense of the world. Design does a similar thing: it makes rough places smooth and habitable, and creates order out of chaos. Design is consequently a happy vehicle for storytelling and in the road layouts, garden design, planting, architecture, allotments, roofscape and footpaths of Applewood, I hope you might recognise something locally distinctive about the place and one day chance upon a corner of it that reminds you of a story within these pages.

As I write, residents are settling in to their new homes, surrounded by landscapers still at work while we beg for patience. Many of the delights and new ideas are yet to be revealed and tested. The 'One Planet Living' objectives that underwrote our design and public realm strategy remain objectives until friendships are made, facilities shared, food is grown and households form that invisible glue between each other – called community. I'm especially impatient to see how the Community Land Trust evolves and matures and how truly socially sustainable Applewood becomes.

It's not surprising that, like planning and building, growing a neighbourhood takes time. However, we can help a little by making the growing conditions right. We can use design to feed the imagination and cheer the heart and we can fertilise the place with stories, history and shared knowledge. In doing just that, this book makes a very important contribution.

KEVIN McCLOUD

Above: Kevin McCloud sharing a joke with Christine Wright, Director of the Cashes Green Community Land Trust, at a tree planting event.

INTRODUCTION

I moved to Stroud in 2006 and living nearby, I frequently cycled past the derelict Cashes Green Hospital site on my way up to Standish Woods, one of my favorite places to go for a walk, run or simply to sit and be still for a while. I knew nothing about the history of the hospital and what it meant to local people. I was curious and was often tempted to jump over the security fences with my camera to explore the dereliction – a photographer's paradise! In 2011 I got wind of the plans to build new homes and attended a community consultation meeting at Cashes Green Primary School. I took my camera of course. I met various project partners and before I knew it, I was fully inducted on the site and given access to document the demolition and the subsequent development. Lis and I already knew each other, but I had not realised how connected she was to the site. Teaming up to write this book was the obvious thing to do.

For me, this book it is the culmination of the story of a very special plot of land. It is not only about bricks and mortar; it is about the 'spirit of place', the relationships between people, and a connection with the earth. Crouching in thick mud, wearing my hard-hat and high-viz jacket, looking, looking again and seeing the colours, textures, forms and light on the site,

I frequently experienced moments of pure bliss. I loved the banter with the builders on site, who I'm sure at times thought I was mad!

Although I am now a photographer, I worked for 20 years previously in community and business development in London, West Africa, and Bristol, hence my deep interest in Cashes Green. I now run Look Again, a business that uses photography to help people see their lives, work and world differently. This book is the perfect coming together of all that is important and meaningful to me – what I refer to as my five Cs: connection, communication, community, creativity and collaboration. I hope it will challenge and inspire future housing developments to look at the gift of land differently.

RUTH DAVEY

Ruth & Lis © Yusupha Davey-Jawara

The inspiration for this book comes from my love of both Art and Place. This interest has come from my family, which is full of designers, architects, artists and musicians. My grandfather was Ove Arup, a Scandinavian civil engineer famous for his involvement in the Sydney Opera House. I studied Fine Art in Context at the University of the West of England and my first project at college was to respond to the closed down Stoke Park Hospital in Bristol. I found it fascinating.

When the opportunity arose to collaborate with another artist, Ruth Davey, and to work in my own community of Cashes Green I jumped at the chance. To document the process of change for this area when the beloved hospital site was eventually to become housing was going to be a challenge. The allotments, which are part of the project, had already been a source of rich history and shattered dreams. The current population in this area live mostly in what is a big housing estate, with small cottages and stone houses which were there before. This is a story of the partnerships, co-operation, idealism, high expectations, good design and new ways of working together. It is also the story of disappointment, lengthy bureaucracy, missed deadlines, frustration and

misunderstandings. It has been a deeply interesting experience and as people come to live here I am excited about how the community will develop.

LIS PARKER

We hope it will become clear as you read the pages of this book, that land – whether it is a modest garden, a park, a piece of common ground or even a football pitch – is more than a mere resource: it is also a place that holds many personal and spiritual experiences that the living beings connected to it resonate with and feel part of. When we change or develop a piece of land, we create a new pathway in its long history, very often bringing to the surface the joy and grief of what was before. Many people, animals and plants have such strong relationships with the Cashes Green Hospital site near Stroud: from the people who have lived nearby for generations or who worked in the hospital that occupied the land for more than a hundred years, to the badgers, slow-worms and apple trees that have thrived in its undisturbed corners and verges.

As the authors of this book, it is true to say that we also felt a strong connection to this place and we wanted to share with you our own journey documenting the transformation of this piece of land in our community.

In Chapter One we have explored the history of the place and how the land was initially developed. Factories, schools and hospitals are continually being created within communities and they provide both work and a social life for the people who live within their boundaries. This particular hospital has been a big part of many people's lives: there were summer fêtes in the grounds and the Randwick Wap – a centuries-old tradition re-enacting a medieval festival – would process through the hospital each year bringing music and ritual to the patients. People who worked there felt part of a healing collective, which had a profound affect on them and their lives. We have listened to the stories of some of those people and have selected a few memorable ones for this book. When you read them in Chapter Two, we hope you will be transported back in time by their story, as we were.

The dilapidated and decaying remains of the hospital buildings – where wildlife ran free and unfettered by human intervention – had to be destroyed completely for the new life of the place to come into being. A period of sadness and anxiety ensued as the demolition team stripped everything down to the bone: old bricks, tiles and chimney pots were taken away to be reused elsewhere and to become part of a different story. The destruction of the old hospital was quite distressing for some

The nurses' home and lodge at the Cashes Green Hospital, circa 1910.

people, dredging up old and sometimes painful memories, but as always, the old must give way to create the new. In Chapter Three you can also experience this transformation through our series of photographs, which hint at the colourful lives and relationships that flourished there over the years.

During the many consultation sessions that were held in the local community centre and school, residents expressed a very clear desire that the old buildings in the hospital should be retained if at all possible, so the decision by HAB to keep the nurses' home and the lodge was well received. The community felt they had been listened to and so went forward with a positive perspective that they were partners in the project. In Chapter Four we show you the 'hands that made it happen' – the workers who came together on the big build.

Since we have been documenting and sharing in the journey of creating new homes in the old Cashes Green hospital grounds, we have relished the moments where the budding community has made time to stop, plant trees, make gardens, and get to know each other whilst crushing apples for juice. These are times of celebration and celebrations are part of the cycle of life.

Through them, we honour the seasons and mark the passing of time by holding events and time-honoured rituals to which we invite friends and neighbours. In Chapter Five we include exchanges and conversations between the project partners who are engaged in coming together to enjoy this place: they tell us how and why they feel it is important to connect with the local community.

We have already mentioned the badgers – they have lived here longer than any humans, together with numerous slow-worms, bats, foxes, birds, mice and other creatures we haven't yet met. They have all had to find their place in the new order that has been created here, but wildlife havens have been a key development priority, so that the wild creatures can live alongside the human intruders, in the gardens, green spaces and allotments. The bats can now roost in an allotment building that has a roof especially made for them. To achieve this wildlife-friendly habitat, the builders were taught about 'One Planet Living' which upholds ten principles for sustainable development, among them the need to protect and restore biodiversity (see Appendix 1). It is great to see the growing awareness on site that we share this land with a myriad of other beings whose right to life we respect. Hopefully, as time goes by and everyone settles into their environs, the new residents will have the pleasure of meeting the old residents who live in the area. In Chapter Six you can hear what the partners are saying about this.

There is a long tradition of 'Land Art' through many cultures across the world, which enables people to express their feelings of interconnectedness with nature. Many of us find that working with nature – through art, gardening, cooking and other creative endeavours – brings an element of spirituality into our lives – it literally grounds us in our being. These varied practices can also be considered as forms of mindfulness, contemplation and meditation. As nature surrounds us and is central to the development of the newly named Applewood site, we wanted to work with the place in a way that would express our love and creativity. So, we held a workshop called 'The Art of Applewood' on a sunny day in May 2014. The participants were representative of existing Cashes Green residents, newcomers to Applewood and the partners in the project. We shared our expertise as artists to inspire each other to take photographs, and make sculptures and installations using found materials.

The results of this incredibly creative and enjoyable day can be seen in Chapter Seven.

It has been wonderful for us to see how the community of Applewood continues to evolve. In a place where individuals came to find solace and support when they were unwell, there is now another, altogether different community, but one that is also built upon a foundation of health and wellbeing. The route is still bumpy in places and there have been cuts and bruises on the way, but the path has been trodden now and for those who wish to live more closely with nature in an urban environment this project has undoubtedly set a precedent, showing others the way forward. In Chapter Eight we discuss the creative and at times challenging cooperation that is needed to bring about projects such as Applewood – a ground-breaking project in so many ways and one that we are so proud to have played a small part in. The project participants are pioneers in 'building for a better world.

The next chapter in this story will be created by the new residents of Applewood.

Hospital to Home

There is a story that needs to be told

About a building that was derelict when sold

It had been a plot of land

Where a hospital would stand

With medicine and fresh air

Doctors and nurses dispensed great care

First they served people who

Had an illness or two

Then nursing the elderly while time passed by

Till they could wave the place goodbye

Closed by those on high

We wondered who would buy

Nature the land began to reclaim

With badgers and bats nothing tame

Years flew past as the dereliction grew

Then at last came along a building crew

They made seventy-eight homes for people like you.

CHRISTINE WRIGHT
Cashes Green resident & Director of the Cashes Green
Community Land Trust

CHAPTER ONE

WHAT WAS

a history of the Cashes Green Hospital

12

In 1892, Cashes Green, a mainly residential area one mile west of Stroud in Gloucestershire, was called the Upper Division of Stonehouse. Lloyd George's map of the area showed there were 85 to 100 houses, all inhabited by persons of the 'working classes'. In 1900 there was an inquiry into the needs for hospitals in the area and eventually a Mr. Booth offered the Old Hill site for a new hospital. The hospital was designed by a local architect, GP Milnes, and built in 1902-4. It opened on 1st December 1904 complete with the most up to date gas lighting. An infectious diseases hospital was then built on the site in 1916 (see page 14 for an article in the Stroud News from 1916).

In the 1930s the Stroud Joint Hospital Board fought off a Gloucestershire County Council plot to rob them of their hospital by the establishment of a countywide municipal hospital service. The clerks 'out letter book' for the 1930's charts the development of local government pensions and as a result we know that there was a matron, two sisters, two nurses, a ward maid, and a porter. From time to time when demand for the hospital was low the Board held posts vacant and actively ensured that additional staff could be called on in an emergency. When a new porter was recruited in 1937 his wife was also interviewed to ensure that she would be a satisfactory temporary worker in times of need. In line with the not so progressive pay policies of our then City Fathers the highest paid member of staff was the porter who also doubled as the ambulance driver! The ambulance appears to have been a Morris Commercial registration number DF8825 supplied by Wycliffe Garage and was used to carry patients to the hospital. It was also used to fetch bedding and clothing for disinfection. The charge for the ambulance was 1 shilling (5p) per mile. By 1937 the hospital had 56 beds and admitted patients with tuberculosis, scarlet fever, diphtheria, typhoid, measles, encephalitis lethargica, poliomyelitis and whooping cough. In common with all hospitals at the time patients were charged for their stay in the hospital with the Poor Law Board being charged for pauper patients. The daily cost was 10/6 (52.5p). This meant that in bad times the charging income covered the cost of the hospital but in good times the ratepayers were being charged for a hospital no one was using.

The coming of the NHS was not welcomed by the Stroud Joint Hospital Board who picked a fight with Nye Bevan to keep the hospital in council hands. They were beaten and the hospital was handed over to the NHS unstaffed and empty with the patients being scattered to Standish and Over Hospitals. The site remained under-occupied for eight years with a small part of the site being used as an annex of Standish Chest Hospital until it was pressed into service to replace the Eastington Workhouse Infirmary Wards as Stroud's Geriatric Hospital in 1956, a service it continued to provide until it was closed in 1993. The allotments next to the hospital, which are on hospital land, were closed in 1997.

The site, including the allotments, was then left empty and derelict. It was transferred to English Partnerships in 2004. In 2005, Gloucestershire Land for People (GLP) set out to try to solve the chronic shortage of affordable housing in Stroud. Its aim was to provide affordable housing under the control of the community and for the benefit of the community, and the Cashes Green hospital site was a possibility. GLP worked with CDS Co-operatives (the largest co-operative housing agency in England) to produce a proposal, which was presented to the Housing Minister in the spring of 2006. After several community consultations, GLP helped set up a Local Partnership Board made up of local residents and stakeholders to

communicate key aspects of the project. Outline planning permission was then granted in November 2009.

In 2012, the developer, Haboakus, a partnership between Kevin McCloud's company HAB (Happiness Architecture Beauty) and developer Oakus (part of the Greensquare Group), won the formal tender for the redevelopment of the site. The Homes and Communities Agency, the government body that owned the land, saw a fantastic opportunity to work with HAB to deliver, "A mixed tenure housing scheme, respecting and engaging with the diverse ecological aspects of the site, to provide an environmentally sound project which actively and positively engaged with local people and organisations", Kirsty Powell, Greensquare Group. The Local Partnership Board with support from GLP, Haboakus, Greensquare and Cainscross Parish Council became a Community Interest Company called the Cashes Green Community Land Trust (CGCLT).

There are now 78 homes on the site, named Applewood, of which 39 are in private ownership and 39 are rented or shared ownership. The CGCLT hold the Freehold Title of the 39 affordable homes. They work in partnership with the Applewood

Cashes Green Tuberculosis Hospital: Opening of the New Buildings

"This week has seen the opening of the Tuberculosis Hospital at Cashes Green, Cainscross and a more comfortable or pleasantly situated building it would be practically impossible to find. It is easily one of the finest institutions of its kind in the county and the Stroud district is well in front of towns in many counties in making so splendid provision for persons stricken with consumption.

The project for the establishment of the institution was first set on foot by the Insurance Commissioners who desired a hospital to serve various parts of the county and one that was centrally situated. Stroud having been selected as the most suitable place, the next step was to obtain a site and after a number of suggestions, a plot of ground adjoining the Isolation Hospital at Cashes Green was found to meet the requirements of the authorities, whose duty it was to superintend the erection of the building. This view was not, as our readers will well remember, held by the Cainscross Parish Councilors, who were supported by the parishioners, and as protest against their district being used as, so they asserted, "a dumping ground." the members of the Council retired as a body.

Consequently, the parish was without a governing body for a considerable time, but during this period and after numerous enquiries had been made as to the advisability of erecting the hospital, building operations were set in progress, with the result that, as we have stated, there now stands a first class institution for the treatment of tuberculosis. Recently the Parish Council has been reformed, and now that the building is completed the Councilors and parishioners can be relied upon to give the hospital all the support possible to ensure its successful conduct."

FROM STROUD NEWS, MAY 1916

Management Company, an estate management company that manages the estate for the benefit of all residents regardless of the tenure of the home they live in. The company has residents on its board and is responsible for the running of the estate, making decisions about grass cutting, window cleaning etc. The CGCLT, which has residents from Applewood as well as other residents living around Cashes Green on its board, provides support around recycling, sustainable transport, and social, educational and community development. This is unlike most private housing developments where residents have no formal voice or engagement in the long-term plans for the environment and community in which they live. The CGCLT is also committed to developing new projects in the surrounding area of Cashes Green with new or existing partners such as the Cainscross Parish Council.

Right: The derelict hospital before demolition in 2012.

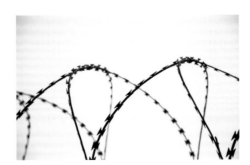

18

CHAPTER TWO

OUR HOSPITAL

stories from those who worked there

RUBY WILLIAMSON

I am Ruby Williamson and I worked for a short time in Cashes
Green Hospital to earn extra money, as you might be sure because
the women put it around that there were jobs going there. I went
down to see the Matron and came away with a job. That was
evenings. I used to go from 7-9. I used to refill the water jugs and
rub the backs and just tidy up the ward and I did that for not all
that long because I became ill. The doctor came to see me and
he stood at my gate and he said, 'Mmm mmm, well I think we
better get you a bed,' and he came back later that day and they
got me into Cashes Green Hospital. So I had to leave my family.

Oh, that awful feeling when you get into hospital when you
start to take your clothes off and you know you are not going to
get them on again for a another 6 months. I just couldn't face it.
I couldn't face up to that. What I did during the course of the
time I was there, I made things, I knitted things. When I was in
the hospital I sent something home every week that I made.
I knitted for the little ones a dolly and a teddy bear. I sent them
home via my husband who came to see me every day. He had to
go through the mill.

Max, my husband, used to drive up with the car and the
children sat in the back and he stopped outside and they stood
up in the car. Then they went 'I have got a new dress'.
Neighbours were so kind they made dresses for them. 'I have
some new sandals'. They stood up in the car and I stood on the
balcony. It seemed as though I was miles away from them but I
wasn't. They were down there and I was up there. It was an open
car they came in and they stood up and they took it in turns to
show me their new dress and new sandals.

Ruby sadly passed away
shortly after the
interview. The framed
photograph of her,
placed here in the
grounds of the hospital
site – with kind
permission from her
daughter Daphne – was
taken by her grandson,
Matthew Archibald, a
Stroud photographer.

DAWN TIMBRELL

I am Mrs Dawn Timbrell. I worked at the hospital in the late 70s-80s. I worked there for 13 years. I went as a domestic but after a couple of weeks I took over and did auxiliary nursing. The people I looked after were bedridden mostly; people who had bedsores or cancer. It was a brilliant hospital, the staff were lovely – a really properly run hospital.

My biggest memory is one about a man that was there whose family lived down in Rodborough and he had lived in Gloucester. One of his brothers still did but the other brother had moved to London and he was coming down the stairs on a double-decker bus and fell from top to bottom and he was paralysed. He went to Stoke Mandeville and the family wanted him to come back down here so they moved him back to Cashes Green. His name was Mr Clark. He was a really nice man and I took him under my wing 'cos I felt sorry for him 'cos he was only 40.

My husband and I used to take him to the Prince of Wales, with permission from the Matron, in a big long wheelchair to get a Guinness 'cos I love Guinness and so did he. And I watched them physio-ing his hands 'cos he used to have a lot of physio, and then I used to do the same for him. Then one day I went in and the Matron called me to the office and then escorted me to his bed where he was laid there laughing. I didn't know what I had done and he literally picked a cup up and drank out of it and he had been able do that for about 6 weeks and he hadn't said anything to me! That was just my way of treating somebody properly. Two months later he passed away. Unfortunately, after that I felt I was taking the work home so I finished but it was a lovely place to work.

The hospital meant a lot to me. The hospital had its own kitchens. Mary Hammond was the head cook there and she cooked there for years. They had an OT place there where they used to go in and do basket weaving and art. I enjoyed every minute of the time I worked there.

22

Dawn is holding a hospital curtain that was found in a bathroom during demolition (see photo on page 39).

LIZ WRAIGHT

I am Liz Wraight and I used to work at Cashes Green in about 1988/1989. The main memory I have of the hospital is the old Nurses' Home. I remember we used the top as our changing rooms. The other buildings were single storey buildings and at the time they were used mainly for elderly people.

I was a qualified nurse, but because I was a bank nurse and so didn't work there all the time, there were other qualified nurses with me who were in charge on the ward. I helped out with the daily care of the patients; lifting them, washing them, and tending to their general care.

My memories of working there are clouded by my own health experiences at the time. I had a back injury whilst working there, so that's influenced my views of it. The work was very heavy. I think things have changed a lot now as nurses have the use of lifting equipment, hoists and other things. I can't recall having this kind of equipment when I worked there, and even if there was, it was hardly used.

Liz is sitting next to a sign found on the door up the stairs in the old nurses' home (see photo on page 44).

TESSA ELAM

My name is Tessa Elam and I am a retired Community Mental Health nurse. I started my training in 1982 and it must have been about 1983/84 when I had my first community placement at Cashes Green in what was the Day Hospital. It was attached to the main General Hospital, what was then known as Geriatric Care. It was a large open-plan room and one end was for people with general health needs and the other end was mostly older people with dementia. I remember it being quite a nice place to work. It was an old building, quite cosy, but it had an air of being efficient and well run. I never saw the Matron, but I am sure she was somewhere there.

We used to have groups and activities and we did art and various creative things. People were there for assessment, as part of the support care plan that they had. There was also an element of respite to give carers a break. I have got very happy memories of my time there especially when the staff had their breaks and we would sit around a big table with a crossword and we would all try and do it together.

I remember there was a lovely garden where the patients loved going for a walk. I remember one particular woman who was always trying to get home to put the chickens to bed and she was quite difficult to manage. The garden was so good because you could just take people for a walk and admire the flowers and distract them and find something interesting to look at. By the time you got back inside they had forgotten what they had gone out for in the beginning. That was a basic skill I learnt at that point.

The hospital at Cashes Green was good because it was something for local people where they could get benefit, be supported and the families were given support too. So it was a very enjoyable happy experience and the big memory I have is it being a very efficient place, small and well run and the staff looked happy. I think Stroud Hospital has still got that special quality which we treasure. A small community hospital. Everybody knows everybody and you get really good service.

26

Tessa with old earthenware pot found in the earth during the demolition (see page 37). Tessa sadly passed away in September 2014. We thank her for her spirit and generosity.

BRYAN KIRBY

Bryan Kirby here. Worked there in 1975 or 76 can't remember. The hot summer anyway. The Area Health Authority ran the area and we were based in Stonehouse, at Standish Hospital so I did one day a week there, the rest of the week I was at Cashes Green Hospital cutting grass, helping out, pruning that sort of thing. The last time I was there was the year I done the Christmas party. They said you're going next week so you can come to the Christmas party. That was the last time.

The garden was traditional lawns and shrubs and winter and summer bedding like sweet williams, wallflowers that sort of thing. They had a new part built – I don't know if anybody knows but, there used to be the TB ward at the very top and just below there they built a new bit, it was probably only a couple of years old when I started there. They wanted a recreational bed, gardens for the residents. So I built a garden for them. They could use it from their wheelchairs. Few trees and a big expanse of grass where they had a fete now and again, which I didn't go to.

I got on well working there. There was a nurse there who lived in the big house, the main entrance – she was the only full time person on site including the matron and that was it, the rest of them came in daily. The matron didn't live there but the nurse lived there in the house but that was the only two full time people basically there. The porters lodge was a cleaning facility and laundry. The place where everybody hid, that sort of place. Not that I went for a fag but everyone smoked in those days. I think they even did on the ward.

I used to feel a bit sorry for the clients because they were basically at the end of their existence. The TB bit had gone. That was where we used to store our tools and all bits of old equipment and then there was a fire next to it. There was an incinerator for the waste in those days, a big fire. I used to feel sorry for them because most were incapable of moving on their own so they used to feed them up and then give them laxatives after they had eaten and by 6 o'clock they were all in bed. It was like the beginning of the end. I felt really sorry for them and the old timers used to come out, hobble out and have a fag and have a chat. It wasn't a nice place to be. I wouldn't have liked to end my days there. Everybody was on pills and given tranquilisers just to calm them down and to keep them calm from the start.

The food was quite nice, the food was traditional. Fish and chips, fish and potatoes on Fridays, that sort of thing, casseroles, proper food. I did every now and again have a lunch but I didn't usually bother. I used to come home early 'cos I had to catch two buses. I wouldn't have lunch, work through lunch and then go home a bit earlier in the afternoon 'cos I was my own boss four days a week. On Thursdays, no Fridays it was, we used to go and pick our money up in a brown paper envelope at Standish as we had to do a day there. It came winter time and I said what do we do now? Cleaned all the tools, got everything ready. Well, whatever the hospital wants you to do. Bit of portering, bit of helping out in the ward now and again, that sort of thing, the rest of the time we were just sitting around reading newspapers and making tea 'cos you couldn't do much in the garden and they had to have so many staff there. There were five including the foreman so come winter time those five people were doing virtually nothing, just pottering around. Done all the painting after a couple of weeks. That was it. I thought, I can't stand this, I can't stand sitting around doing nothing, so I gave in my notice and said bye bye. That was winter of 76. Nice year!

28

Bryan is holding an old
cigarette packet found on
the hospital site during
demolition. He used to
smoke this particular brand.

30

CHAPTER THREE

HOSPITAL NO MORE

the demolition

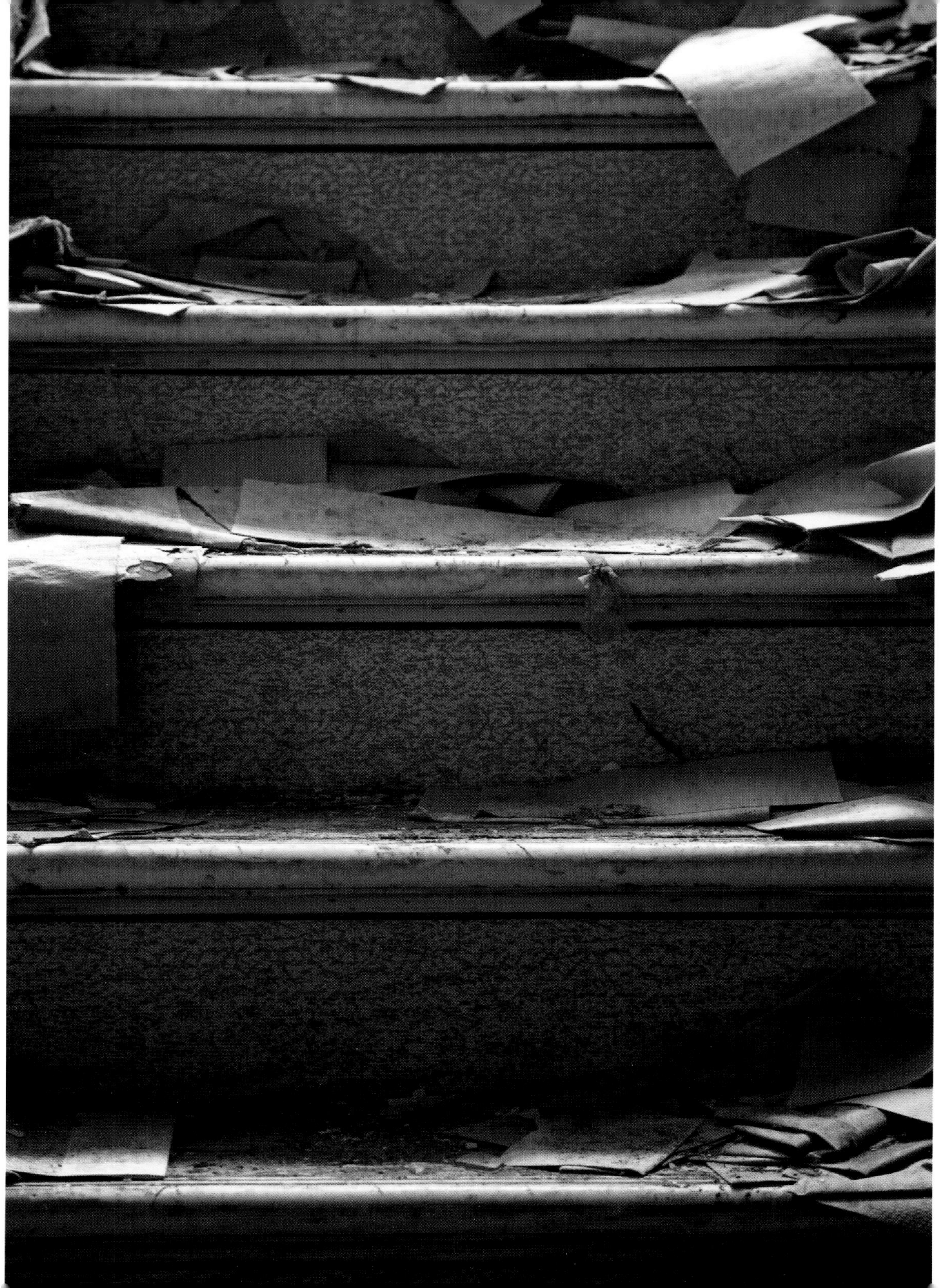

PLEASE CLOSE THIS DOOR

12:30 NOON

THANK YOU

DO NOT OPEN

CHAPTER FOUR

BUILDING NEW HOMES

the hands that made it happen

BUILDING NEW HOMES

The building of the Applewood housing development has been an experience quite different to that of most other new housing projects. In this chapter, members of staff from the contracted companies involved, tell their stories.

Dennis Higgs, Site Manager, Markey Construction

There have been a lot more environmental considerations on this job than usual. We expanded our normal induction to incorporate these environmental aspects, which were a sizeable part of it, and it has really paid dividends. We ensured that we left the bits of green space that are being preserved on the site as undisturbed as possible, protecting them from all the building work. The environment we've got, we've got to look after! We've devastated 90% of the site – but that's the nature of building: it's got to go, but the pieces we've kept we have put a lot of time and effort into keeping untouched. For bricklayers, framers and young people learning the trades, it's good for them to see a working site and how it all fits together. Maybe the younger ones will get inspired! We've accommodated school visits, college workshops, even work-experience groups from Belgium. This is a lot more than we would do on a standard project. We always score well on the Considerate Constructors'

Scheme, but this project has given us a chance to push those boundaries even further.

Dalton Cullen, Contracts Manager, Markey Construction

Applewood has been designed and built to the highest specifications around a 'fabric first' principle to improve energy efficiency. So, the houses are extremely thermally efficient, using a simple heating system in a super-insulated building envelope with high performance windows. It has been awarded the Code for Sustainable Homes Level 4.

Sarah Button, Community Development Manager, Markey Construction

For me it's about getting the sustainability message across to the lads on site. I'm especially happy that they have been so receptive to the One Planet Living framework and the environmental induction. Having them help out rescuing bats and slow-worms has been great. It's good to see the environmental message getting through! The building industry is responsible for almost 30% of the UK's carbon emissions and so it's a really good place to start addressing our environmental impact. It's such a large industry that it can be clunky and slow to change, but projects

like this one that take the time to introduce everyone on the site to the sustainability goals will really make a difference: if you can get all the labourers on board, not just the companies at the top level, it seems like a small thing, but over time the positive effects will add up.

Dominic Fitchett, Senior Commercial Manager, DBK Partners
It is the mindset and approach that has really made this scheme different: from the respectful way the site has been used – retaining the Victorian nurses' home and lodge together with the stream and established trees, to providing high quality shared space and ensuring that all homes, whether outright sale, shared ownership or for affordable rent have been integrated to sit side by side with each other to create a real community.

We are fully committed to engaging with local communities so throughout this project we have sought to appoint local suppliers and tradesmen and encouraged the Greensquare 4ward2work scheme. This meant we provided employment, training, education, work-experience and apprenticeship opportunities on site for local schools, scout groups, colleges and the unemployed in the Cashes Green and Cainscross area.

Of particular interest in this project was the provision of a new community building for the allotments and a new kitchen for the Youth & Community Centre.

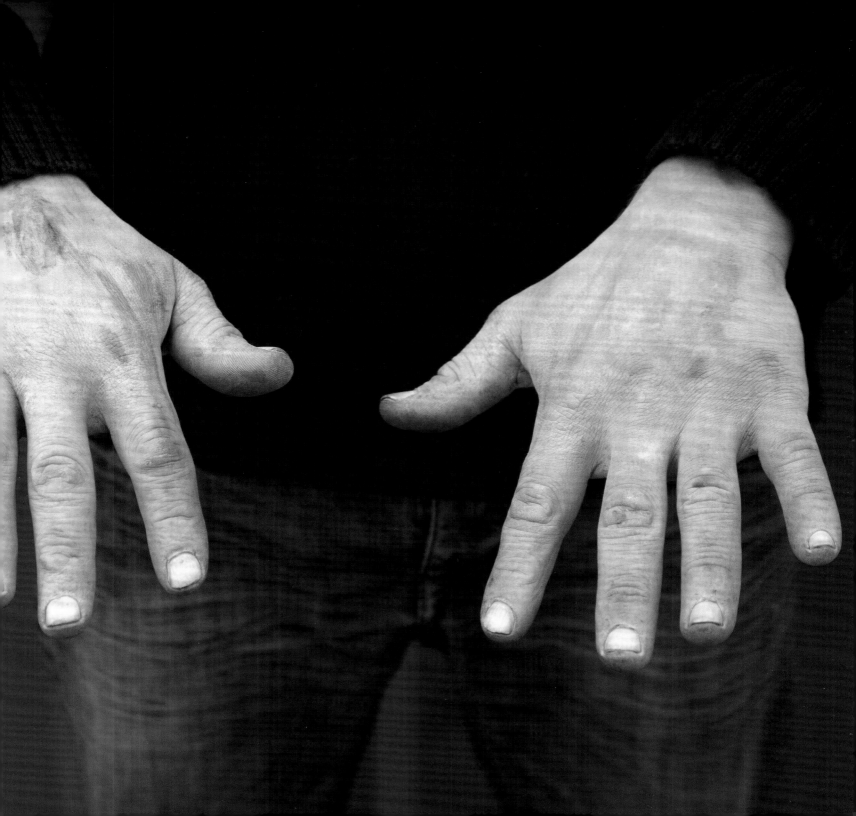

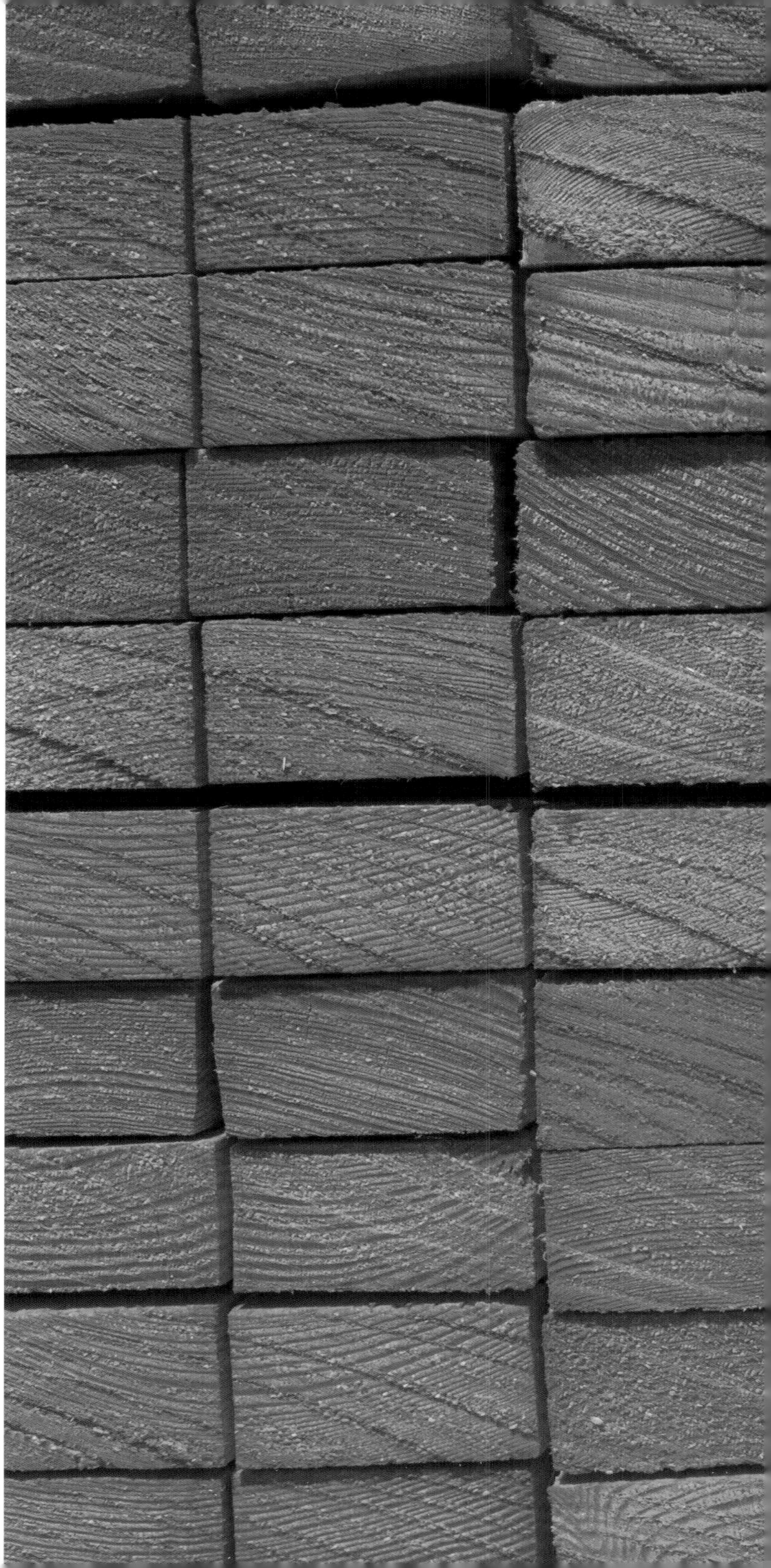

Taking recycling seriously,
both in terms of encouraging
all building staff to recycle
their day to day 'rubbish'
and by re-using building
materials wherever possible
or selling them on to
recycling companies.

64

CHAPTER FIVE

BUILDING FOR PEOPLE

engaging with the community

66 Engaging with residents of Cashes Green has been of major importance to the building of Applewood. Here, the project partners tell their stories.

Mike Roberts, Managing Director, HAB

Trying to get local people to feel that this is a positive addition to the neighbourhood and not just a load of houses being foisted upon them, is the big challenge – alongside trying to maximise local residents' participation in the scheme.

Jeni Marshall, Clerk, Cainscross Parish Council

The Cainscross Parish Council is the first tier of government and therefore closest to the community. We have been involved from the initial concept of Applewood and as elected representatives of the local community felt our input was essential for our parishioners. There have been many challenges, partly due to the amount of organisations involved in the project, but now with residents moving into Applewood, we look forward to seeing a blossoming new community, integrating with the existing communities of Cashes Green. One of the Council's main ambitions is to bring the allotments back into use and we hope to see them fully up and running by the spring of 2015.

Kirsty Powell, Development and New Business Manager, Greensquare Group

Haboakus took on board comments from local residents in shaping its detailed planning application and final scheme. This meant that Haboakus took the specific decision to save two of the popular old hospital buildings from demolition, the Nurses' Home and the lodge, which was welcomed by all and ultimately brings a sense of place, context and history to the new development. The Cashes Green Community Land Trust worked with Haboakus to interview and select the main contractor to build the new development. It also helped shape the Local Lettings Plan agreed with Stroud District Council which sets out how the homes will be occupied and suggested the final adopted street name: Old Hospital Lawn.

David Hills, Director, DSDHA Architects

Every decision has been made with the residents in mind: to build a community and opportunities to interact with neighbours. The close dialogue with landscape has established a comfortable relationship with the surroundings, so there is a bigger emphasis on shared space than you usually find in this kind of residential community. It is a new type of sharing: in the

A community celebration with tree planting and a visit from Kevin McCloud.

gardens, the green 'wildlife spine' and also, the allotments.

Max Comfort, Co-founder and Chair, Gloucestershire Land for People
We have sought from the beginning to involve the local community in decisions over the future of the hospital site and were running community consultations years before Haboakus came on the scene. I have been saddened by the sometimes cavalier and very disrespectful way that some of our alleged partners have treated the Cashes Green community, such as information being withheld or delivered late. The community has, in my view, been treated as a poor relation and with distrust. It has not been an equal partnership by any means.

Sarah Button, Community Development Manager, Markey Construction
My priority has been sharing the construction process with the community as much as possible, and trying to make sure that the lines of communication stayed open, by making sure that regular updates went out through the newsletter and the noticeboard, but also that I was keeping in touch with the CLT as much as possible in between those updates. It has been brilliant to visit the local schools and then have them come back and visit us on site. We've had so many groups through; a really diverse lot. The relationship with Cashes Green Primary has also really flourished, and I'm so pleased that we've been able to keep that going throughout the project. Ultimately this is not really 'our' site or 'our' project – we are just here for a little while, building it. It will ultimately belong to the community and the people who move in. There is already an incredible sense of community here in Cashes Green, and I hope that we can help foster and facilitate a sense of pride in the new houses, and a sense of people having been involved and included along the way.

COMMUNITY LAND TRUST
Find out more

DROP-IN SESSION
TODAY
3:00 - 7:00 PM
ALSO
SITE VISITS
ENQUIRE WITHIN

Consultation and information events were held at the Cashes Green Primary School and community centre. Local residents, school children and groups of people from near and far, were invited to visit the site during the building process.

Builders and visitors
alike were kept updated
about environmental
commitments and
community events.

Members of staff from
Greensquare kept
people happy at a drop
in event held at the
community centre.

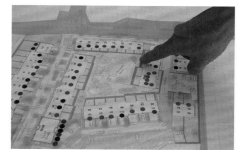

Members of the Cashes
Green Community Land
Trust pose for a celebratory
PR opportunity!

CHAPTER SIX

BUILDING FOR THE PLANET

considering the site's ecology

78

Environmental considerations have also played a major part in the Applewood development. Here, the project partners share their stories.

Mike Roberts, Managing Director, HAB

HAB tries to help people make sustainable choices more easily. We take a rounded approach to environmental issues and try to avoid any 'eco-bling'. Maintaining a rich local ecology is a very real challenge at Applewood, but accommodating the badgers, bats and slow worms along with all of the other flora and fauna is a challenge we relish.

Kirsty Powell, Development and New Business Manager, Greensquare Group

Haboakus employed a firm of ecologists to work with the design team to provide advice and guidance right from the very early stages of the project. Before any work could start on site a large population of legally protected slowworms had to be captured and relocated into the allotment part of the site. This can only be done during the active season so the timings of the capture process had to be carefully planned into the overall construction programme. A long established badger set was protected and retained in the estate design. A feature was made of an existing watercourse across the site. Existing hospital buildings were carefully stripped to protect the local bat population and new bat boxes were erected on trees and new bat habitats designed into the scheme. 15 new allotment plots were brought back into use for food growing early in the summer of 2011, three years prior to completion of the whole development. Haboakus also employed a firm of energy consultants to work with it on the sustainability aspects of the new homes. We have used a 'fabric first' approach i.e. super insulating the new properties, and the consultants provided advice specifically on the type of heating and ventilation system to use in all the homes. The planting strategy across the site also places emphasis on edible plants and on biodiversity in general, rather than purely ornamental planting and growing.

Max Comfort, Co-founder and Chair, Gloucestershire Land for People

Affordable housing is not just about the cost of the build: it is also about the affordability of use – the fact that people on low incomes can enjoy a lower than average electricity bill or have access to cheap electric bikes. I am pleased that Haboakus have placed a strong emphasis on the 'fabric first' approach to building, focusing more on high levels of insulation and airtightness

rather than on what can sometimes be token 'eco-bling'. The retention of the allotments was one of GLP's key priorities, along with the promotion of edible landscaping, very much in synch with the 'One Planet Living' approach advocated by Kevin McCloud.

Paul Menzies, Director, Curtins
We were keen to review the site infrastructure and look at methods to reduce carbon both through construction and in use. Our integrated highway and drainage solution has reduced the amount of underground drainage pipes which in turn has reduced construction activities and materials, enabling a reduced maintenance regime as the drainage network is visible from the surface and therefore easily inspected and maintained. We have also utilised a 'swale' (an area of land that absorbs and dissipates water) within the allotment area that is fed with surface water from the site. This helps attenuate the discharge of rainwater from the site but also aids irrigation on the allotment area through local sumps built into the system.

Luke Engleback, Founder/Director, Studio Engleback
We call this the 'eco-urbanism approach' – a whole system approach where landscape is certainly not a 'prettifying' feature,

but the central issue; 'landscape led urbanism' you might say. It is a form of 'biophic' design and planning: a green infrastructure that delivers a series of green services. From these functions we get the aesthetic. We wanted a people-oriented place that at a wider scale connects communities, because previously, this site had been a closed space. It was important to all concerned that the allotments were conserved by the site planning and re-established before demolition of the old hospital building. Whilst we all enjoyed the ephemeral delight of the birds and butterflies on site, there have been challenges presented by the protected species – the bats, slow-worms and badgers, but ultimately, biodiversity is so much more than protected species: it is also fundamental in underpinning our lives, as 70% of the food we eat needs pollination. We need to reconnect with nature, a process that has been eroded over 200 years of increasingly urbanised living.

David Hills, Director, DSDHA Architects
It is not about green bling, but rather the basics of engaging with nature: to feel a sense of wellbeing; and creating good environmental awareness in terms of design – such as looking at where the sun rises and falls, or where the shadows will be, in order to define good spaces to sit in and to socialise in.

View of Selsley Common
beyond the community
allotments. A barrier
was erected to protect
the slow worms during
the building process.

Fruit trees in the old
orchard adjacent to the
allotments. Carefully
designed and landscaped
communal spaces run
throughout the site.

84

CHAPTER SEVEN

THE ART OF APPLEWOOD

seeing the extraordinary in the ordinary

THE ART OF APPLEWOOD

The Art of Applewood workshop is an important part of our story. Right from the beginning it was essential for us to provide an opportunity for existing residents of Cashes Green, new residents of Applewood, and project partners to interact with each other through art.

We based the workshop in the ecological corridor of the site, where nothing had changed since the building began. We sat in stillness and silence on the earth, closed our eyes and allowed ourselves to breathe deeply. We listened. We smelled. We tasted. We felt. We opened our eyes. We looked again. We saw the colours, textures, shapes and forms in front of us. Seeing with new eyes, we explored the rest of the site, discovering the extraordinary in the ordinary. We gathered grasses, flowers, sticks, stones, building materials and rubbish. We took photographs and created art from what we found.

This is what the participants said:

"I liked the freedom to explore, to use different materials. I was really impressed with the peace of the site."
Lou Perry, local Cashes Green resident

"This has been a wonderful way to connect to the site. A lovely way to explore the peaceful and wild spaces."
Tom Beer, Applewood resident

"I enjoyed exploring the wildlife." **Lola Beer (8), Applewood resident**

"I enjoyed finding out about the Applewood site beyond the buildings and connecting with the community more."
Ed Staff, Applewood resident

"A lot of what I've done on this project has been 'outward-facing'. Today was a nice change, and a chance to make some tiny moments of meaning and leave a little ephemeral piece of myself on the project. Such little things make a building site into a home and community."
Sarah Button, Community Development Manager, Markey Construction

Workshop participants look again at the site and make temporary pieces of land art out of what they find.

Next page: Photos © Ed Staff (left), © Tom and Kate Beer (right).

Photo: © Tom and Kate Beer

Photo: © Lis Parker

This series shows Ruth's
love of how building
materials relate to
nature through colour,
texture and form.

CHAPTER EIGHT

BUILDING FOR A BETTER WORLD

a creatively challenging collaboration

Applewood project partners shout about their successes and admit to challenges encountered along the way. Recognising there are lessons to be learned, they offer suggestions as to how this project can be used to influence policy and practice when building houses for the future.

David Warburton, Head of Area, Homes & Communities Agency

This is the first time a Community Land Trust housing project has been delivered on Homes and Communities Agency owned land in England, and we have developed different ways of working to support this process. This project feels like a natural part of Cashes Green. This is important to us because we want local people to have a strong connection with the site, as they had when it was a hospital. We worked hard to fully engage the local community and selected a partner in Haboakus who shared our commitment to this. Community engagement doesn't finish with the completion of the development. The Community Land Trust and the estate management arrangements in place will ensure that the local community continues to have a say in the future of the site for years to come. The design, quality and 'look and feel' of the new homes are second to none and it really feels like a place, not an ordinary housing estate. I'm really pleased that when you

drive to Applewood it feels like part of the neighbourhood that has naturally evolved. It has been challenging doing things which are not conventional, in terms of some highway and planning aspects. It's been great to have the cooperation of the local authority in pushing the boundaries here with things like the edible landscape, communal garden and Home Zone areas. This means we have been able to deliver a scheme that ordinarily would not have been achieved. It's important not to be formulaic and just look at the textbooks, but rather to develop a place which takes its lead from the site and feels a natural part of area.

Mike Roberts, Managing Director, HAB

In physical terms, saving the two hospital buildings is the single biggest result. They speak of the history of the place and root the scheme firmly. Otherwise, just getting to know a range of local people who care deeply about their place and receiving their input has been invaluable. The biggest challenge has been trying to please all of the people all of the time, which as we all know is impossible. We have little expectation of influencing housing policy at present, but hopefully Applewood can inspire changes in practice. We are constantly seeking to put people even more at the centre of new developments and hope that our custom build offer will help this.

The project was imposed on the community by the HCA who wanted to try out a Community Land Trust project to see if it was viable and could be rolled out nationally. Although it has turned out reasonably well, the community had no say in this decision. The success was primarily in ensuring that the site did not fall into the hands of developers whose sole purpose was to exploit it for profit and thus the fact that some beautiful homes have been built where otherwise run of the mill 'executive homes' might have been spawned. The high level of affordable homes (50%) and the fact that this was achieved with no state subsidy is an example to the world that we can dismiss the bleating of speculative developers who complain they cannot afford to build affordable homes.

Max Comfort, Co-founder and Chair, Gloucestershire Land for People
Another success has been that we were a bit of a 'thorn in the side' of myopic bureaucracy in demanding clarity and integrity. One of GLP's key successes has been in supporting a local community with a long history of being 'done to', in rising to the challenge of taking on the responsibility for owning an important local asset and in becoming fit for purpose – supporting the local Cashes Green community in gaining a

measure of respect from the other partners in the project. This has been the greatest struggle, against a deeply embedded culture that holds community groups to be incapable and unprofessional, and that volunteers cannot be trusted with 'real' projects. We have balanced our support for the local community with allowing it to take risks and develop responsibility.

By far the most important lesson however is one still to be learned by our partners: to trust the good intentions of the community; to acknowledge its strengths and skills and to show it the respect normally accorded to a partner. A personal lesson for me is to be far more demanding earlier on in projects and not to believe that large organisations automatically contain wisdom when they often don't. For the Cashes Green community, I'd like to think the lesson is also to be far more demanding of its partners, to shout louder and be aware of its own many strengths.

There are aspects of this project that should and already are influencing practice: the lack of a need for government subsidy, and the particular and very successful approach to design set out by Haboakus are but two examples. It has, however, not been a community-initiated project but rather, plonked on Cashes

Key players in the
Applewood development
who have also supported
the making of this book.
New residents start to
build relationships with the
land and each other.

102 Green from on high, thus rather ironically repeating history. It is testament to the power of community and some of its major players that Cashes Green saw through this early on and decided to have none of it. Finally I would like the true story of this project to be one that encourages other communities to take their destiny into their own hands and never take "No!" for an answer.

Paul Menzies, Director, Curtins

This scheme looks at construction, operation and communities in tandem, to ensure the right solution has been developed and has not been afraid to challenge industry standards in looking for new methods of construction and community living.

David Hills, Director, DSDHA Architects

Defining a streamlined client and community group would ease decision making. This project demonstrates the need for specific design solutions for unique sites to build on qualities, thus avoiding 'cookie-cutter' types of layouts that are generic and not 'of the place'. There is no fast-track to getting it right but the hurdles to gain approvals for compliance with generic standards almost deny the opportunities which can be exploited with creative thinking. Less red tape is needed to enable good design

to be executed by committed clients.

Dominic Fitchett, Senior Commercial Manager, DBK Partners

There are two key lessons that should be highlighted. Applewood has shown that the Code for Sustainable Homes Level 4 Standard can be met by paying attention to detail during the design and construction process. This includes meeting stringent targets for insulation and airtightness rather than bolting-on renewable technologies. Secondly, the level of consideration paid to the external space was as much as that given to the internal space: from the Home Zone traffic management to the communal gardens and retained wild areas. We hope that this design focus is repeated in future schemes.

Luke Engleback, Founder/Director, Studio Engleback

This project must change policy. We will constantly strive to do more with less, to be true to eco-urbanism and the tenets of a 'One Planet Living' approach. We don't have an alternative.

Denis Higgs, Site Manager, Markey Construction

The environmental aspects for me are more about social sustainability. This comes down to the level of integration with

the local schools, colleges and community. The fact that Markey employed a Community Development Manager made a big difference. Normally, this aspect would be a small part of the build and the site managers would squeeze it in where they could.

Sarah Button, Community Development Manager, Markey Construction

I think that there are community engagement and communication aspects of this project that should be tried everywhere! People tend to think of sustainability as being made up of wind turbines, solar panels, bats and badgers – but there is also a huge social and community aspect that is often overlooked. These are the things about local economy, involvement, and community ownership that we've tried to focus on in this project. Thinking about 'big picture' sustainability instead of focusing just on the ecological aspects is another thing I'd like to see more of in the industry.

Peter Allen, Director, Cashes Green Community Land Trust

Most local communities have very little influence over new housing developments. With Cashes Green Hospital being a central landmark, community involvement from the very early planning stages was important and will help make Applewood a success. Maintaining

as much of the ecology and green space as possible has been key to the Cashes Green Community Land Trust. Returning the allotments to fruitful production and provision for the existing wildlife has been our fundamental objective. Seeing the development going ahead and meeting most of the original objectives is the proof that this type of joint development can work.

Looking back, the hurdles that we as a group have faced with little previous experience have at times been overwhelming. Achieving 'fit for purpose' status and developing a working relationship with Greensquare, the developers and the Homes and Communities Agency has at times been difficult.

Many lessons can be learned: better understanding about the relationship between the groups involved and their priorities; understanding key requirements that need to be in place to allow a successful outcome; keeping to the original idea that attracted you to become involved in the first place. I would like the lessons from this development to influence housing policy and practice. Having existing residents actively involved in housing developments within their community is important and should be a key factor at the early planning stages of any new developments.

The community centre
(on the left) hosts the
'Welcome to Applewood'
residents' party in
September 2014.

Dawn Timbrell cuts the 'Welcome to Applewood' cake. The old nurses' home has been restored and transformed into six flats.

THE 10 PRINCIPLES
of ONE PLANET LIVING

1
Zero Carbon
Making buildings more energy efficient and delivering all energy with renewable energy.

2
Zero waste
Reducing waste, reusing where possible, and ultimately sending zero waste to landfill.

3
Sustainable transport
Encouraging low carbon modes of transport to reduce emissions, reducing the need to travel.

4
Sustainable materials
Using sustainable healthy products, with low embodied energy, sourced locally, made from renewable or waste resources.

5
Local and sustainable food
Choosing low impact, local, seasonal and organic diets and reducing food waste.

6
Sustainable water
Using water more efficiently in buildings and in the products we buy; tackling local flooding and water course pollution.

7
Land use and wildlife
Protecting and restoring biodiversity and natural habitats through appropriate land use and integration into the built environment.

8
Culture and community
Reviving local identity and wisdom; supporting and participating in the arts.

9
Equity and local economy
Creating bioregional economies that support fair employment, inclusive communities and international fair trade.

10
Health and happiness
Encouraging active, sociable, meaningful lives to promote good health and well being.

113

LIST *of* SUPPORTERS

We would like to thank the following companies and organisations
for their support in funding this book and providing invaluable advice
and support in its production.

Homes and Communities Agency

www.homesandcommunities.co.uk

HAB

www.habhousing.co.uk

Greensquare Group

www.greensquaregroup.com

Cashes Green Community Land Trust

www.cashesgreenclt.org.uk

Markey Construction

www.markeyconstruction.co.uk

Gloucestershire Land for People

www.gloucestershirelandforpeople.coop

Cainscross Parish Council

www.cainscross-pc.gov.uk

DSDHA Architects

www.dsdha.co.uk

DBK Partners

www.dbkltd.com

Curtins

www.curtins.com

Studio Engleback

www.studioengleback.com

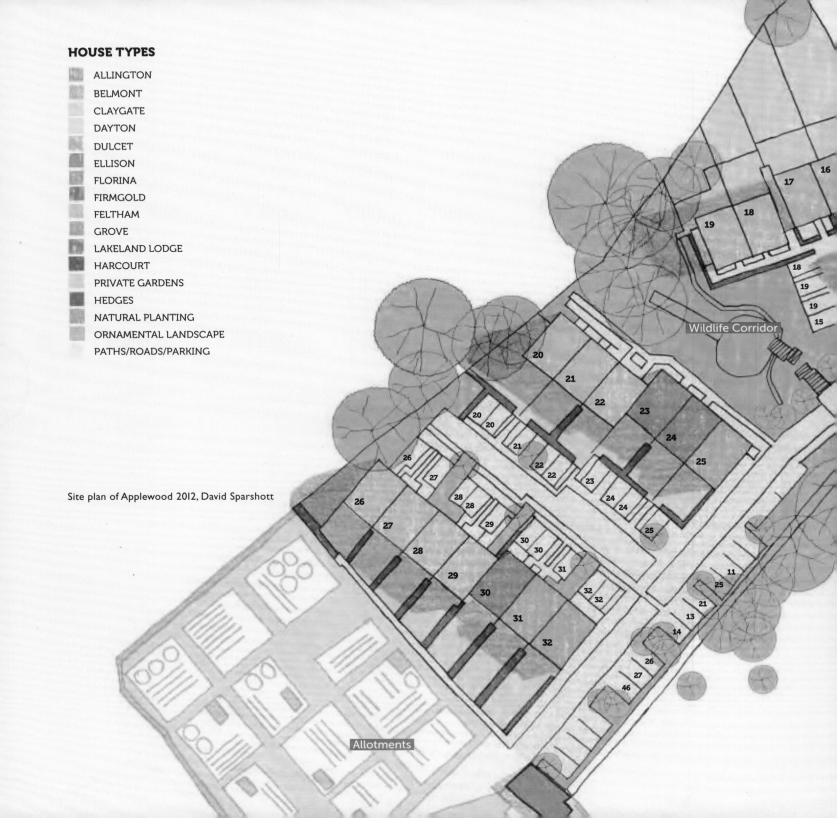

HOUSE TYPES

- ALLINGTON
- BELMONT
- CLAYGATE
- DAYTON
- DULCET
- ELLISON
- FLORINA
- FIRMGOLD
- FELTHAM
- GROVE
- LAKELAND LODGE
- HARCOURT
- PRIVATE GARDENS
- HEDGES
- NATURAL PLANTING
- ORNAMENTAL LANDSCAPE
- PATHS/ROADS/PARKING

Site plan of Applewood 2012, David Sparshott

Wildlife Corridor

Allotments